D1422811

LEICESTERSHIRE WATERMILLS

'Sence' Flour Bag

NORMAN ASHTON

LEICESTERSHIRE WATER-MILLS

27 OCT 1980

Y4 ,8642

UNIVERSITY LIBRARY
4 JY 1978
CAMBRIDGE

SYCAMORE PRESS
WYMONDHAM
LEICESTERSHIRE

Copyright © Norman Ashton 1977

PRINTED IN ENGLAND

my Folly

for my Father (1906 — 1975)

ISBN 0 905837 02 9

First published by N. D. Ashton, 1976
in a limited duplicated edition
for private circulation, under the title
IN SEARCH OF LEICESTERSHIRE WATERMILLS

THIS EDITION
Published by

SYCAMORE PRESS LTD

WYMONDHAM
MELTON MOWBRAY
LEICESTERSHIRE

CONTENTS

ACKNOWLEDGMENTS

I would like to take this opportunity to record my thanks to the owners of local water-mills and local people who gladly gave of their time to talk about the mills.

Also, my thanks to the following for records, old photographs and prints:—

Loughborough Local History Library;
Leicestershire Records Office;
Leicestershire Museums (Newarke);
Leicester Reference Library (Local History);
Mr. Lloyd Tomlyn (Mountsorrel Mill);
Mr. R. Sharman (Barrow Mill);
Mr. Warrington (Eye Kettleby Mill);
Miss G. M. Vice (Blaby Mill);
A Mr. Cable who many years ago kept a scrap album of items of Leicestershire interest;
Mr. Nigel Moon for access to his notes and photographs.

And last, but not least, my thanks to my wife for many patient hours of typing.

INTRODUCTION

The history of milling is irrevocably intertwined with the history of civilisation. The invention of such things as the steam engine, the petrol engine, the aeroplane or television are seen by many to be the only benefactors of mankind, forgetting that the inventors of the water driven corn-mill have a strong claim to have influenced man's progress to a greater extent than any other single invention, for from that time the supply of the basic need of life, food, could be regularly maintained.

It is a sobering but warming experience to stand outside an old mill on old grinding stones laid down successively over the years as flagstones, stones which, who knows, were grinding when Richard III fell at Bosworth Field. The sight of these stones can set one pondering, blurred visions of those sturdy millers of so long ago, generation upon generation, a continuity all should realise and cherish, a reminder that time moves relentlessly on.

The attraction of water-mills that led to my search can, I hope, be appreciated — the direct thread to ages gone by.

I was disappointed not to find some literature about Leicestershire water-mills, so that as my search progressed I realised that my researches, if of a somewhat amateur nature, could be of interest to other similarly minded people. I therefore resolved to publish a record of my findings.

Having completed this most enjoyable task and glancing back through the pages, my rambles do not sound like very much at all, but I at least am left with a great deal, the memories of places I will in all probability never visit again, and which have become part of my inner memory, to be recalled and dwelled upon on occasions that require perspective and the assurance of the uncorruptibility of time and the relative insignificance of daily events.

As this book is aimed primarily at those who may not already be familiar with water-mill technology, Part I of this book is devoted to a

general survey of water-mills, their history and technology. It is hoped that this will provide a background against which Part II, concerned solely with Leicestershire water-mills, can be better viewed.

I hope the reader will forgive the more obvious inadequacies of this publication and have their interest whetted enough to pursue this part of our heritage further. It is a matter of regret, I think, that no Leicestershire water-mills are preserved in public hands for the enjoyment of future generations.

Finally, I would be very pleased to receive any further information/photographs/postcards relating to old Leicestershire water-mills that the reader might have or know of.

N.D.A.

Grinding Stone Manufacturers

OPTIONAL

PART ONE

A GENERAL INTRODUCTION
TO WATER-MILLS

Chapter One

A BRIEF HISTORY OF WATER—MILLS

The water-mill was for over 1,000 years, until the introduction of the windmill in the 12th Century, the only form of mechanical power available — the water-mill and windmill then being the unrivalled providers of power for a further 600 years until the introduction of the steam engine in the 18th Century.

The Greeks are credited with the invention of the first water-mill, being mentioned by Antipater of Thessalonica in about 85 B.C. The early Greek water-mill, however, was not one we would easily recognise today, the wheel being set in the horizontal plane, rather than the vertical water-wheels which became common in this country. The invention of the vertical water-wheel is generally attributed to Vitruvius, a Roman architect. Although Vitruvius's mill is mentioned as early as 20 B.C. there is no record of its use until 320 A.D. The first conclusive documentary evidence of a water-mill in England is taken to be 762 A.D., when reference is made to a water-mill in connection with a monastery. An earlier claim is made for Ireland in 651 A.D., with a reference to the mortal wounding of two brothers at a mill.

It is not until 1086, however, that a clear picture emerges. The Domesday survey shows that some 5,624 mills were present in England in 1086 — this suggests a remarkable growth in the building of mills during the two preceding centuries. The number of sites would have been somewhat less than the above figure, as clusters of mills occur with as many as 15 mills on a site or settlement. These early British water-mills were of low power and are assumed to be of the horizontal Greek type, because of their relative simplicity, although it is probable that some were of the vertical Roman type. Each mill, it is calculated, had to supply an average of 50 households. Although it is generally accepted that the mills were used for grinding cereal crops, evidence exists to suggest that a few were employed on other uses, such as grinding metal ores. Many Domesday sites were used down the years for successive structures, but only one mill (Guy's Cliffe in Warwickshire) has Saxon workmanship in the existing building.

The mills, almost without exception, were to be found in the South and East of Britain — Norfolk (537 mills), Lincolnshire (436 mills), Wiltshire (390 mills), Somerset (351 mills) , and Kent (334 mills) being particularly well supplied. Turning to our particular area of interest — Leicestershire — 123 mills are listed on 89 sites or settlements.

Passing on from Domesday, for several hundred years after, the Lord of the Manor dominated mill life and history. The owners of ancient manorial mills possessed 'soke rights', which meant that anybody requiring corn to be ground, however small the quantity, had to take it to the Lord of the Manor's mill. This caused considerable ill feeling by tenants — well recorded in many disputes — and also led to the unpopularity of the miller. The 'soke rights' continued right up until the 19th Century, the last being Bradford, which obtained release in 1871 from this unfair ancient system.

As the supply of water was essential in this highly profitable trade, many lawsuits resulted from disputes between mill-owners concerning restrictions of water flow, etc., so much so that it was written in the early 19th Century:—

'In consequence of so many water-mills, the country is never free from litigation and vexations, lawsuits respecting erecting, repairing or raising weirs, by which the peace and harmony of neighbours and friends are often destroyed.'

During their early history, water-mills were used primarily for agricultural purposes, i.e. irrigation and cereal grinding. It was not until around Domesday times in this country that other uses began to be found, as individual millers adapted the power for peculiarly local uses. One of the first alternative uses of water power was the grinding of iron ore, for in the Domesday survey a few mills are valued in 'blooms of iron'. By the middle of the 16th Century in Britain, water-mills were used in the processing of iron, providing power for the bellows of early blast furnaces, and forging iron, using the tilt-hammer device, as used by the fullers.

A major development in the use of water-mills was at the end of the 12th Century, for 'Fulling' or 'Tucking'. Fulling is the process of treating loosely woven cloth in water to shrink and thus improve it. For this purpose the rotary movement of the wheel had to be converted to a vertical striking action. This vertical motion was also used in the process of tanning (or dye making) from the early 13th Century, when trip-hammer devices were used to crush tan-bark to produce dye, and later woad, which produced blue dye. By the early 14th Century, there were a number of mills grinding ochre and even wood.

11.

The ingenuity of man put this power to many other uses, amongst which are recorded:— saw-mills, paper-mills (including Laverstoke which made paper for the Bank of England), gunpowder-mills, boring-mills (i.e. gun barrels, etc.), water pumping-mills, silk-mills, cotton spinning, snuff, oil, leather and numerous other uses, many of which are now long forgotten.

At the beginning of the 19th Century developments occurred which spelt the eventual death-knoll of water-mills. These were, firstly, steam driven mills, followed closely by steel roller mills. The output of these inevitable successors could not be matched, either in output or cost, by the smaller water-mills. It is surprising however, how long some of these small mills survived. Many smaller mills continued to compete by installing the more efficient water turbine, or installed steam engines to ensure continued output when lack of water would normally stop grinding.

The decline did not really take a grip until the end of the 19th Century. The decline in Leicestershire is illustrated graphically in Chapter 3, and shows that country mills managed to keep going until the turn of the 20th Century in roughly the same numbers, but then declined rapidly until, in the present day, no water-mills now grind in Leicestershire. The rate of decline would be similar throughout the country, although some mills in England still grind flour for the health-food trade, and some still grind animal foodstuffs.

The day of the water-mill is over, but meanwhile the natural successor to the ancient mills, the hydro-electric power station, provides power to modern industry in a true linear descent from the earliest simple Greek mills. These too, however, seem doomed to be overtaken by Nuclear power, but at what cost? The water driven power station provides, in addition to power, water for domestic and irrigational purposes — the Nuclear power station provides power, but leaves a legacy of waste material that will poison for untold centuries to come.

Chapter Two

WATER-MILL MACHINERY

As mentioned in Chapter 1, the first water-mill is accepted as being the Greek mill. This type of mill, which was of simple construction, had a horizontal wheel and no gearing. As can be seen from Fig. 1, the water reached the wheel down a wooden trough (A), hitting the wheel (B) which was in a horizontal position. The wheel shaft (C) passed through the bottom grinding stone (D) and was fixed to the upper grinding stone (E) which thus revolved at the same speed as the wheel, the bottom grinding stone remaining stationary.

This type of mill found its way to Britain and, although superseded by the Roman mill in England, was used until fairly recent times in Ireland and Scotland, where it was known as the Norse mill. It is the Roman mill of Vitruvius, however, with its vertical wheel, that we recognise as the forerunner of the typical British water-mill. Fig. 2 shows a diagramatic representation of Vitruvius's mill.

The vertical water-wheel is fixed on the axle (A), on to which is fixed a toothed drum (B), which is in the vertical position. This toothed drum meshes with another toothed drum (C), which is in the horizontal position and free to revolve. Thus the rotation in the vertical plane is converted to rotation in the horizontal plane. The horizontal drum (C) is fixed to a vertical shaft (D) which passes through the bottom fixed grinding stone (E) and is attached to the top mill-stone (F). Thus the bottom stone remains stationary while the upper stone revolves and provides the grinding action. The speed of the stones could be altered to suit local conditions (i.e. speed of the stream) by varying the relative number of teeth and the diameter of the toothed drums (B) and (C).

Vitruvius's mill became the model for water-mills as we know them. His design was so simple and so effective that relatively few improvements have been made in the 2,000 years of its life. The first major improvement, introduced during the 16th Century, was the move from a single pair of stones to the driving of two or more pairs, by introducing spur gearing on the main vertical shaft.

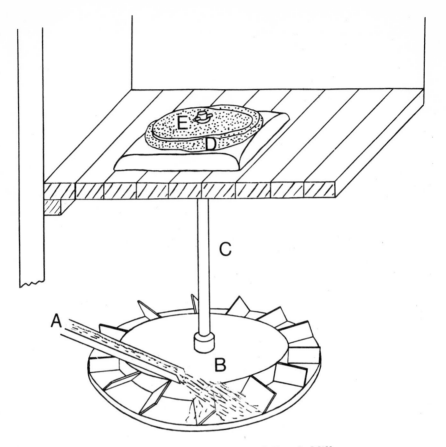

Fig. 1 — Diagrammatic representation of Greek Mill.

Towards the end of the 18th Century cast iron was introduced into mill machinery and at the same time experiments were carried out on the design of wheels. John Smeaton (1724 — 92) brought many improvements to the water-wheel in the late 18th Century and also covered many other aspects of the working of water-mills.

Here it is appropriate to look a little more closely at the working of a water-mill, starting at the storage and control of the 'essential ingredient', water, to the types of water-wheel, and lastly, a look at a 'typical' water-mill's internal machinery.

Firstly then, we look at the method of raising the power that turns the wheel. The first need is a fall of water to create the force or energy, which is captured by the wheel and conveyed by means of gearing to the grinding stones. The storing of this power is essential so that the

14

miller, with planning, can control the rate of water-flow. In this respect the water-miller has a great advantage over the wind-miller, who obviously cannot store his source of power. The general means of storing the water power was by constructing a dam in the form of a weir, which maintained the water level, while a sluice-gate controlled the water entering the wheel. Sometimes a sluice-gate acted as the weir, the level of water being built up, say overnight, to be utilised during the day by means of another sluice-gate guarding the entrance to the wheel. However, as with the machinery inside the water-mill, the methods employed outside are equally varied and dependent upon local circumstances. Figs. 3 and 4 show 'typical' arrangements.

Having established a store-house of power, there are a number of ways of utilising it, depending on the fall of water available. Where the fall of water is small an Undershot Wheel is used (Fig. 5). The early water-mills were of this type. This utilised the force of the water striking the bottom of the wheel and was relatively inefficient due to water losses at the sides of the wheel and the effect of water below the wheel working against the rotation of the wheel. They were also subject to fluctuations in water flow. (See photograph on page 58).

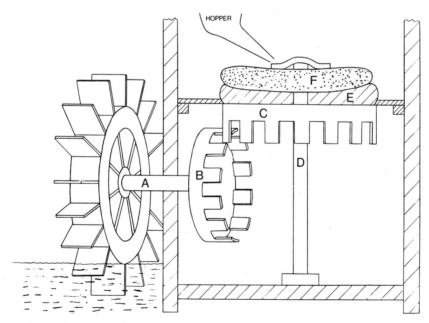

Fig. 2 — Diagrammatic representation of Vitruvius's Mill.

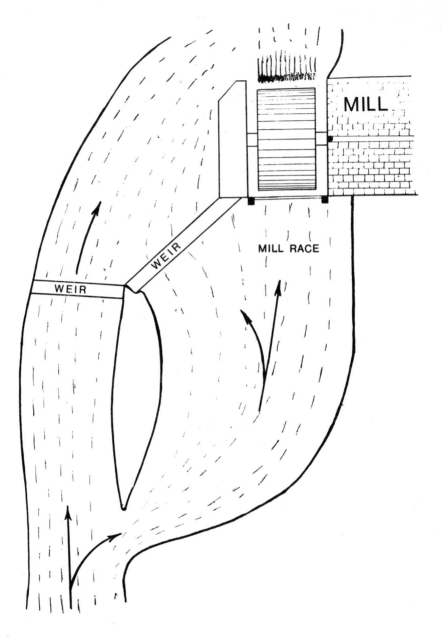

MILL

WEIR

MILL RACE

WEIR

Fig. 3 — Example of Mill water flow.

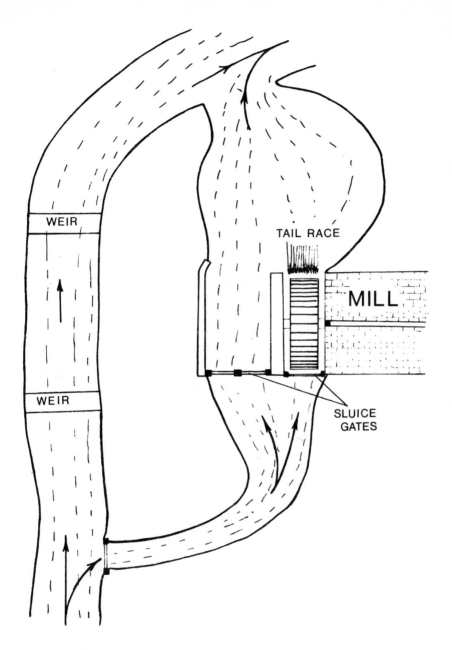

Fig. 4 — *Example of Mill water flow.*

UNIVERSITY LIBRARY
DUPLICATE
B
4 JY
1978
CAMBRIDGE

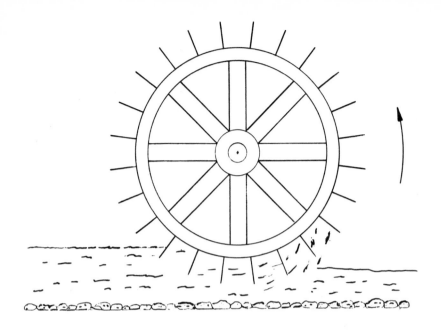

Fig. 5 — Undershot wheel.

J. V. Poncelet introduced a considerable improvement to the undershot wheel during the early 19th Century and the wheels were called after him, Poncelet Wheels, (Fig. 6).

Since the efficiency of the undershot wheel depended on the effect of striking the wheel vanes. Poncelet redesigned them so that water entered and left the wheel without shock, thus using all the power for turning the wheel. He also reduced the 'drag' tendency by having no bottoms to the buckets. These were referred to as ventilating buckets.

Where the fall of water was sufficient, the Overshot Wheel was used, being introduced during Roman times.

The overshot wheel depends on the weight of water instead of velocity, the weight of water in each bucket helping to turn the wheel. In general, the larger the diameter of the wheel the faster the speed it revolved at. Its main advantage over the older undershot wheel was that it required far less water. Its disadvantages were, a) as it required a larger fall of water the sites were less plentiful; b) because the water had to be taken over the top of the wheel the construction was far more difficult and expensive; and c) because the direction of flow in the tail-race was opposite to the direction of rotation of the wheel, an effect called

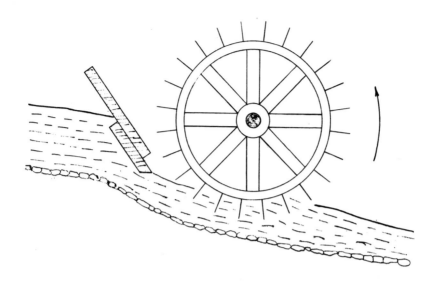

Fig.   6 — Poncelet wheel.

Fig.   7 — Overshot wheel.

'back watering' could occur, which reduced the power of the wheel. To overcome the effect of back-watering the Pitch-Back Wheel was introduced. (See photograph on page 46)

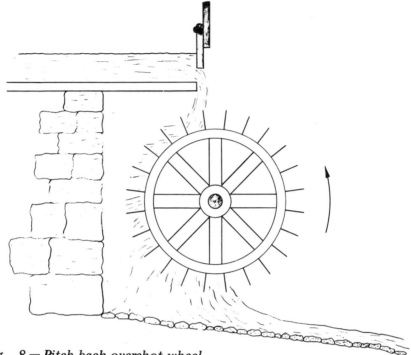

Fig. 8 — Pitch-back overshot wheel.

Here the water was introduced to the wheel before the top (on the 'near-side'). This reversed the direction of rotation of the wheel to conform with the tail-race flow direction, thus acting with, rather than against the flow, and so increasing power.

The third main type of wheel, the Breast-Shot Wheel, was not introduced until the 16th Century. Although named breast-shot because the water, in theory, was introduced to the wheel level with the wheel axle, in actual fact this varied, sometimes being above the axle and so called high-breast, or below the axle and called low-breast. The efficiency of the breast-shot wheel depends on the ability of the buckets to hold the water for as long as possible while at the same time releasing the water as quickly as possible at the bottom of the wheel. It is this final type which was most commonly used during the 19th Century, due to its relatively high level of efficiency against cost.

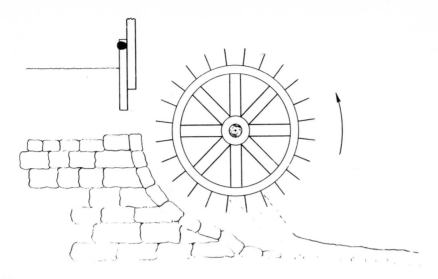

Fig. 9 — Breast-shot wheel

Having looked at the source of power and its method of generation, we look finally at a typical water-mill's internal machinery.

Fig. 10 shows a diagramatic representation of the main gearing in a typical later water-mill. Although the gearing is very much the same in all water-mills, the auxiliary gearing will vary enormously according to local requirements and the particular miller's ingenuity. The water-wheel (A) is connected by means of a shaft to the Pit-Wheel (B) which usually has bevelled teeth. This meshes with the Wallower (C), also usually with bevelled teeth. This converts the vertical rotation to a horizontal rotation. The wallower rides on the Main Shaft (D). Parallel to the wallower on the main shaft is the larger Spur Wheel (E), which in turn engages with the smaller Stone-Nuts (F), both having vertical cogs. The stone-nuts ride on a small vertical shaft, supported below, which passes through the stationary Bed-Stone (G) and is fixed to the Runner Stone (H). The bed-stone remains stationary, the runner stone, as its name suggests, revolving, thus creating the grinding action. At the top of the main shaft (D) is the Crown Wheel (I) which returns the horizontal rotation back to vertical rotation by means of a bevelled cog (J) — this rides on a horizontal shaft (K). On this shaft various pulleys are located, from which the mill's accessory equipment is run. This would include, sack hoist, threshing machine, flour grading equipment, saws, tool grinders, etc.

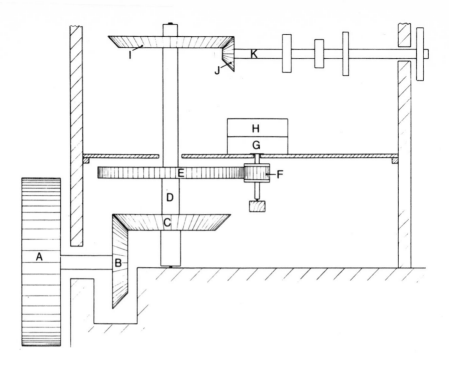

Fig. 10 — Typical mill gearing arrangement.

Should any reader not familiar with water-mills have had his interest sufficiently aroused, I can do no better than direct him to the three books mentioned at the end of this chapter. Apart from the excellent content of these books, the bibliographies of John Reynolds' and Leslie Sysons' books are comprehensive and should furnish the reader with hours of further enjoyment.

British Watermills by Leslie Syson, Published by Batsford (1965)

Windmills & Watermills by John Reynolds, Published by Evelyn (1970)

History of Corn-Milling: Vol. II Watermills & Windmills
    by R. Bennett & J. Elton, (1899) (Reprinted 1975)

PART TWO

LEICESTERSHIRE WATER-MILLS

Chapter Three

LEICESTERSHIRE WATER-MILLS

It has been suggested that the first water-mill in Leicestershire was sited at Croft, the word being derived from *Craeft* whose meaning in old English was 'a machine, or engine'. As this village is known to have been in existence in 836 A.D. it gives Croft a substantial claim to the title. It seems more likely, however, that the water-mill arrived in the north east of the County from Lincolnshire, which had one of the greatest density of mills in the Country. It is not just coincidence either that the north eastern part of Leicestershire was a great cereal growing area, which could support a denser population and the cost of constructing mills.

In general, the siting of the first mills must have been governed by three factors:

  (i) population density;

  (ii) nearness to cereal growing areas;

  (iii) a stream with sufficient fall of water to power a mill.

The Domesday survey shows us in detail the distribution of mills in Leicestershire in 1086 A.D. (Fig. 11). Although there are minor discrepancies in the survey, it nevertheless shows quite clearly the situation.

It can be seen that, using the River Soar as a dividing line between the east and west of the County, the eastern half has a large number of mills in contrast with the western half of the County which has relatively few. The highest concentration of assets, both natural and man-made, was in general found in the eastern half. Ploughs, meadow-land, rivers/streams, all these interdependent assets, allied with the growth in the use of the water-mill from the eastern side of the County, make it not surprising to find the Domesday map showing such a sharp division in distribution of mills. At the time of Domesday, for example, approximately two-thirds of the population of Leicestershire lived east of the Soar and about one-fifth to the west of it, the remaining population being, in the main, situated in the Soar valley. As the population at

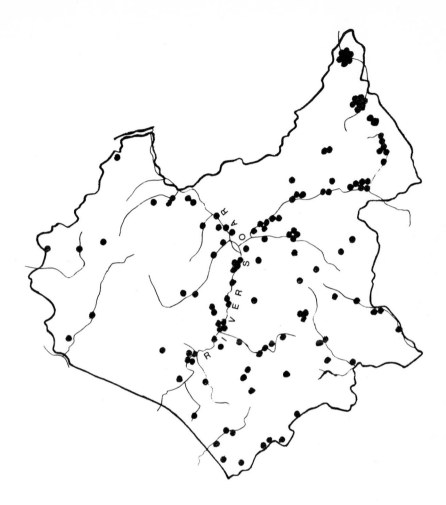

Fig. 11 — Distribution of mills in Domesday times, 1086 A.D.

that time would tend to gravitate to the areas of greater natural abundance, this illustrates the advantage the east of the County must have had over the western half.

No other major reliable survey incorporating water-mills, covering the whole of Leicestershire, was done until John Prior surveyed the County for his map published in 1779. This is particularly useful as it is towards the end of the 18th Century that the decline of the water-mill started, and so shows the distribution of water-mills before the decline. Fig. 12

Fig. 12 — Distribution of mills on J. Prior's map, 1779.

shows the distribution, which can be readily seen to have shifted quite significantly from east to west during the 700 years since Domesday times. It would be extremely interesting to trace the distribution of mills during this intervening period. It would seem probable that during the period up to the 14th Century there was an increase in the number of mills generally, but proportionally more in the west of the County (this following the trend in population). From the 14th Century onwards, the eastern uplands, with increasingly more permanent pasture, became an area of low population density and it is probable that about this time we began to lose the numerous mills in the east which appear on the Domesday map, but not on Prior's.

By the end of the 17th Century, the density of population in east and west was equal. The expansion of the coal-mining and other industries during the 18th and 19th Centuries finally took the population the complete circle with the west becoming more densely populated than the east. The concentration of the east on stock raising and dairying, with the introduction of more powerful mills and improvement of transport, will have further contributed to the decreasing number of mills in the east. What is particularly noticeable is the polarisation of mills by Prior's time to the main rivers and tributaries, reflecting the need for more power to drive the much larger mills being introduced.

Although by 1779 the actual number of mill sites had decreased from 89 to 78 on Prior's map, in terms of output a huge increase had been effected; whereas in Domesday the 123 mills meant 123 pairs of grinding stones, the mills in 1779 would almost certainly have had at least two pairs of grinding stones of much larger diameter than those used in Domesday times, and of much greater efficiency.

The distribution of mills seen on Prior's map in 1779 is the distribution recognisable well into the 20th Century, although the number of mills declined.

From 1779 it is fairly easy to trace the decline in the number of active water-mills, using maps and trade directories. Fig. 13 shows a graph of the number of water-mills from 1779 to 1970. It can be seen that the water-mill, although losing ground steadily, held out well against the introduction of the steam powered roller mills until quite late in the 19th Century. Some mills found other uses for their power and so survived that way. It was the thirty years from 1890 — 1920 which really spelled the end of the water-mill in Leicestershire. Floods, war and financial pressure all played their part, indeed it is somewhat of a surprise to find so many surviving into the 1930's. Many had, of course, traded their wheel for a turbine, or added a steam engine, to increase power and efficiency. One of the last commercially worked mills, Help-out Mill, which finished in 1970 after the death of its owner, Mr. Timms, converted to a turbine in 1902 — a fact which is proudly displayed on a plaque above the mill door.

The big mill at Sheepy Parva added a steam engine around 1895, followed by a turbine, and in the early 1930's converted to electricity. Rearsby had a steam engine from the late 19th Century, although the chimney has now been taken down. Soar Mill at Sutton Elms had steam at the beginning of the early 1900's, but had reverted to water power only by 1908, and remained so until it closed in the late 1930's. It is interesting to note that at Mountsorrel the steam engine was used in times of flood to pump the excess water away, rather than as direct power to the mill, thus enabling the mill to keep functioning. Steam engines were often used as indirect power, for example acting as a pump to re-circulate water from the tail-race back to the mill race, thus ensuring a constant supply of water to the wheel.

Of the thirty-one or so mills operating in the 1930's only ten survived into the second half of the 20th Century, and of those only three made it to the 1960's, so that by the time of compiling this brief record, no water-driven mills operate - the last links of an almost two thousand year tradition cut.

Thus we have almost covered the full circle in the life of water-mills. Water-mills are, fortunately for them, nearly always sited in beautiful places with the sound of falling water, usually in a valley of trees with relative peace, and so many will survive for many more years by nature of their beauty and associations, by being converted to private accommodation. Cossington Mill, for example, has been converted into a fine restaurant, which draws people from all over the County to 'prop up' the bar, which once propped up the grinding stones.

If sometimes the building will not survive, the associated waters, particularly the mill-ponds, will live on, guarded jealously by the ever-swelling numbers of anglers. This is not a new use for the waters, however, eel-catching being one of the 'perks' of the miller in ancient times, when eels were common fare. Much sport was also provided as the following list of catches testifies:—

1811 Dishley Mill	— 2 Pike over 25lbs.
1845 Barrow Mill	— Pike, 33lbs.
1888 Aylestone Mill	— Roach, 2lbs. 2oz.
1892 Thrussington Mill	— 2 Bream, 5lbs. 5ozs., 4lb. 3½oz.

But what of the men who worked the mills, an often insular breed by nature of geography, the mill usually being sited away from the village or town. Many names crop up again and again in mill records and show the long linear tradition of some families in milling covering many generations — one of the longest being the name of Timms at Help-out Mill. The line finished with the death of Mr. Elijah Timms in 1970, but started well over 300 years ago at Ashby-de-la-Zouch, and established itself at Help-out Mill, Odstone in 1734. In the early days, of course, the miller was only a tenant, but gradually the millers became owners and prosperous and respected members of the community. The mill at

Odstone was bought by Mr. Samuel Timms in 1818, along with 152 acres of land, for £1,000 and the mill remained in the family right up until 1970.

Many other families have a tradition in milling and amongst the names that crop up are:—

Archer, Berridge, Bowley, Chester, Cooper, Cufflin, Draper, Everard, Fawkes, Graves, Goodacre, Halford, Haynes, Hives, Jelley, Robinson, Slater, Stretton, Timms, Wall, Walters and Wright. The names crop up in early conveyancing documents, in sale catalogues and in 19th Century trade directories, like the Goodacres in the late 19th Century, when in 1887 the conveyance of Desford Mill lists the brothers John Goodacre (41 years) of Nutbourne Mill, Pulborough, Sussex, Joseph Halford Goodacre (40 years) of Loughborough, miller, and Tom Goodacre (34 years) of Desford, miller, all being sons of John Goodacre of Desford Mill, who was miller at Desford from 1818 until his death in 1871. The Desford Mill remained in the Goodacre family until early in the 20th Century; the name Goodacre being carried on in conjunction with another milling name, Everard, at Lower Mills, Loughborough, up to the present day.

An interesting miller was Gerald Chester who worked the mill at Belton until his premature death in the early 1950's, caused by a lung complaint due to the flour dust. He had only one leg and must have had some difficulty moving about the three-storey Belton Mill.

Thomas Haynes was one of the longest serving millers at any particular mill - he worked Clock Mill in excess of 52 years. Mr. Haynes came from a milling family, being born at Southam Mill in Warwickshire, his parents coming from the famous Chesterton windmill reputedly designed by Inigo Jones. Several other members of his family were also millers. The last miller at Claybrooke Mill, Arthur Tyers, was first mentioned in 1895 and was still listed in 1941, so could have exceeded Thomas Haynes' fifty plus years. William Stanton of Market Bosworth Mill was in residence at his mill for over 73 years, up until the late 1920's, his family having come to the mill around 1830.

Many of the millers changed mills several times in their lifetime and sometimes took on two or more mills at the same time. William Chester was shown in White's Trade Directory to be miller at Thringstone in 1877, Worthington in 1894 and Belton and Worthington in 1900. Shepshed Mill had nine millers between 1828 and 1936.

Many stories abound about millers, mainly centred around their supposed dishonesty, made immortal by Chaucer's 'The Miller's Tale'.

In those distant days when millers took a part of the flour as payment, this reputation may well have been deserved. I prefer to see them as a special breed of men with rare ingenuity, in fact the first engineers and if not the fathers, then the grandfathers of modern industry.

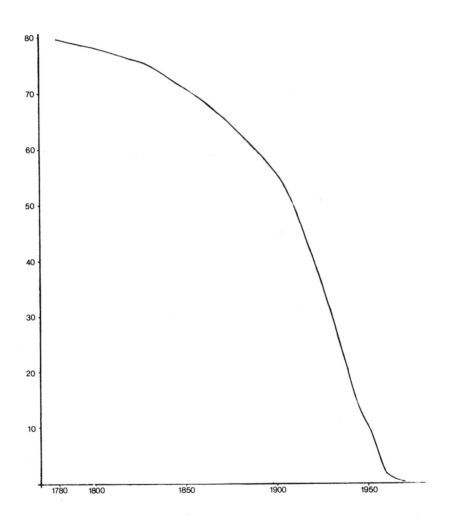

Fig. 13 — Graph of number of mills during period 1779 — 1970.

Chapter Four

SURVIVING LEICESTERSHIRE MILL BUILDINGS

As far as I was able to find, forty-three mill buildings still survive in Leicestershire, none, unhappily, still working. Several of these mills still have all or part of the mill machinery intact and a few more still have all or part of the wheel, while most have old grinding stones in the vicinity. They now have a variety of uses — eighteen have been converted to private houses, one is a restaurant, eight are just storehouses, one is used for industrial purposes and two, Broughton Astley and Sheepy Magna, are still grinding using modern machinery. The rest are empty and unused, several being in a dilapidated condition.

I sought out over seventy mill sites which references showed could still be standing. The search took me hundreds of miles to places I would never otherwise visited or stumbled upon, isolated places, as many Leicestershire mill sites are. They have given me many memories to mull over — the flashing blue of kingfishers near Ravenstone and other mill sites, a rabbit chasing a stoat near Syston, a deserted swan's nest at Sileby, the birth of a calf near Rearsby Mill, the quiet and relaxation of falling water where the mill stream and weir still survive.

The following chapter is a small amateur salute to these survivors of time, progress and sometimes indifference — forty-three mill sites as I found them. At first sight some may look like ordinary, though unusually designed, private houses, but a second look betrays the telltale signs of their former associations. Long may they survive.

ALLEXTON MILL

Allexton Mill is situated just inside the eastern county boundary on the picturesquely twisting Eye Brook.

Two mills are listed as part of the assets of Adelachestone (Allexton) in the Domesday survey, one of which is quite probably the same site as the present mill building.

The mill is not listed after 1912 in the Kelly's Trade Directory and so, presumably, ceased working soon after.

The mill and mill-house have been converted over the last twenty years into a private dwelling, the mill formerly being in a dilapidated state.

The wheel, which was of the pitch-back over-shot type, was quite large, being 8—10 feet wide, and all wood — the wheel axle lies in a field nearby.

AMBRO MILL, WILSON

Ambro Mill is hidden down a private road just outside the village of Wilson in the north west of the County.

Known in earlier times as Handbarrow or Hanborrow, Ambro Mill has a long pedigree, being mentioned in regard to the transference of the tithe of the mill in about 1240 A.D.

The oldest part of the present building is about 500 years old, with further parts about 300 years old. When the mill was converted into a private dwelling a large beam was retained, bearing several items of 18th Century graffiti, including the initials TA, followed by the date 1732.

The mill had an all iron over-shot wheel and the source of water power was the Ramsley Brook, which eventually finds its way to the River Trent.

ANSTEY MILL

First mentioned in 1306, Anstey Mill stands on Rothley Brook (originally known as Hathebrook), just outside the village. The present building is of red brick with a slate roof and three floors — it was probably built in the early 19th Century. The mill was mentioned in trade directories until the early 1920's when, presumably, it fell into dis-use, now being used as a store. The iron wheel has now been removed but must have been 12 — 13 feet diameter and of the low-breast type.

When a lease was drawn up between Robert Martin, owner, and Shirley Wain (miller until 1904) in 1872, the schedule of the mill was:—

    2 pairs of French grinding stones
    1 pair of barley grinding stones
    a dressing machine
    smut machine
    sack tackle
    chains
    iron waterwheel and gearing.

ASHBY FOLVILLE MILL

Ascbi (Ashby Folville) is mentioned in the Domesday survey as having a mill, and nearby Gaddesby is also mentioned as having two and a half mills, so it is likely that the present mill building is on one of these ancient sites.

The mill drew its water from the Twyford Brook, a tributary stream of the River Wreake, but the large mill dam pond has long since been dry, as the mill ceased working about 100 years ago.

The wheel, which was probably of the over-shot kind judging by the height of the mill-pond, was situated at the left-hand end of the mill, as is evidenced by the 'peeping' mill-race exit at the bottom of the photograph.

Interestingly, the remains of a windmill are within a stone's throw of the water-mill, which would have provided alternative grinding power.

BELTON MILL

Belton Mill was amongst the last working mills using a water-wheel in Leicestershire. It would have been very well known in days gone by, because the Great Horse Fair of Belton was sited in a field opposite the mill — the Fair drawing large crowds from a wide area. The mill was apparently involved in the apprehending of a thief who stole money from the Fair. He was making his getaway down the mill tail-race culvert when the miller was shouted to open the sluice-gate — this he did, and the unfortunate miscreant was arrested in a rather soggy and undignified manner.

From 1900 the mill was worked by successive members of the Chester family, Gerald Chester being the last miller at Belton.

The mill, which was always involved in grinding cereals, had three pairs of stones, which were turned by an over-shot wheel. The wheel has now been removed. In the latter years of its working life, until its closure in the late 1950's, only animal feed was ground.

BILSTONE MILL

Bilstone Mill is picturesquely situated on the River Sence, West Leicestershire (i.e. not the River Soar tributary). It stands about two miles up-stream from Temple Mill at the northern end of the village.

The wheel and gear have gone, although remnants of the gear can be seen in the mill. The breast-shot wheel must have been 4—5 feet wide and 14—15 feet in diameter and drove two pairs of stones.

The mill building looks to date from the 18th Century, the attached buildings probably being added in the 19th Century.

The mill was still listed in Kelly's Directory in 1941 and was still believed to have been grinding grist into the 1950's.

BLABY MILL

This fine old mill is situated on the 'other' River Sence, a tributary of the River Soar, well hidden off the track leading past Blaby Cemetery.

Bladi (Blaby) is mentioned in the Domesday survey as having a mill, which was quite probably on the same site.

The mill, in common with several other Leicestershire mills, had auxiliary steam power, as evidenced by the large steam stack. The machinery has long since been removed, the mill not having been worked since 1926.

A bridge over the nearby Union Canal is called Vice's Bridge after one of the former Blaby millers, whose family worked the mill for over 100 years.

Although the miller's house which was attached to the mill has been demolished, members of the last miller's family still live at the mill cottage behind the mill.

Blaby Mill c.1880's, with the Vice family posing outside.

BROUGHTON ASTLEY MILL.

Brostone (Broughton Astley) is mentioned in the Domesday survey as having a water-mill, the present mill building being situated on the southern fringe of the village near the church.

The mill was powered by water until 1945, when it was converted to electricity — the old water course and sluice gate can still be seen. The old mill building, built in 1803, is largely engulfed by modern additions, but the old section can be seen on the photograph above.

Mr. Pickering, the owner of Broughton Mill, formerly had Stemborough Mill, the next mill up-stream from Broughton Astley on this tributary stream of the River Soar.

The mill still operates, grinding cattle foods using modern machinery.

CLAYBROOKE MILL

This fine old water-mill lies on a source stream of the River Soar, about a half-mile outside the village of Claybrooke Magna. The site dates from the 13th Century when there was a water-mill and windmill, the latter having long since disappeared. The present mill building dates from the late 17th Century.

The mill ceased operating as a mill, using auxiliary power, on Coronation Day, 1953, the wheel itself having ceased to turn some time earlier.

Most of the machinery is intact and is found at the right end of the mill building. The wheel, although dilapidated, is still there — the fact that it is made from wood perhaps saving it from the scrap metal fate of many of the iron wheels. It is of the pitch-back over-shot type, 11 feet in diameter and 5 feet wide. The wheel drove two pairs of grinding stones, as well as many accessories, via a lay shaft on the first floor. Many of the mill accessories are still there, albeit a shade dusty.

*First floor, Claybrooke Mill, showing the main-shaft,
bevel-geared crown-wheel and grinding tun.*

Bevel geared pit-wheel engaging with the wallower; the spur-wheel sits above — Claybrooke Mill.

Stone-nut engaging with the spur-wheel — Claybrooke Mill.

Crown-wheel and spur cog on the lay shaft which drove the mill accessories — Claybrooke Mill.

CLOCK MILL, MEASHAM

Clock Mill stands just off the road leading through Swepstone to Ibstock and drew its water from the curiously named River Gilwiskaw. Equally curious is the origin of the name, Clock Mill — whatever it is is lost in time gone by.

The mill dam was built in the 16th Century but the mill had evidently been rebuilt and raised prior to 1874, when Mr. Thomas Haynes renovated the mill, before going on to be miller for over 50 years.

The water-wheel, of the over-shot pitch-back type, 11 feet diameter and 6 feet wide, still lies in the wheel-house. The wheel drove two pairs of grinding stones, one of which is still in place in the mill, as is most of the other machinery.

The mill was still grinding animal feedstuffs up until ten years ago, as the great-grandchild of Thomas Haynes, who now lives at Clock Mill, informed me.

The overshot pitch-back wheel at Clock Mill.

COSSINGTON MILL

One of the best known old water-mills in Leicestershire, Cossington Mill has a long history. The current buildings date from the early 17th Century, but the site was first mentioned in 1248 A.D. and is thought to be one of the three Domesday mills associated with Barrow-on-Soar.

Originally a corn-mill only, by 1477 it was described as a corn and fulling mill, but by the end of the 15th Century it had probably reverted to corn grinding only. By 1657 the mill was described as a corn and paper mill; this dual role continued for nearly 200 years, when it once again reverted to the occupation of corn grinding. The last miller, Henry Gardner, left Cossington Mill in 1928 when the machinery was removed.

The mill had an under-shot wheel, which was housed in the small wheel-house on the right of the building, and drew its water from the River Soar.

In 1928 the mill was purchased and extensively renovated by Mr. and Mrs. Pick, who then opened it as tea-rooms until, in 1967, it was re-opened as the now widely acclaimed Cossington Mill Restaurant.

Cossington Mill c.1904; the millpond is now a car-park.

CROW MILL, SOUTH WIGSTON

One of the better known former water-mills, Crow Mill (at one time referred to as Union Mills) is situated just south of South Wigston on the Countesthorpe road.

Although not a Domesday Mill, it must have appeared on the site shortly after, as a mill was mentioned in the middle of the 12th Century. Evidence of the earlier stone buildings can be seen at the bottom of the present mill building.

In keeping with the dishonest tradition of millers, Crow Mill features in Court Rolls during the 16th Century, when two of the millers were found guilty of taking excessive tolls. One of these millers, Roger Langton, was the first of three generations of Langton's who worked Crow Mill well into the 17th Century.

The mill was not mentioned in Kelly's Trade Directory after 1900, when it was listed as being steam and water driven and worked by William Vice who also worked Blaby Mill at that time.

Crow Mill, early 1900's, with Miller Redhead outside.

DESFORD MILL

Desford Mill ceased operating as a mill in about 1922, nearly 800 years after having been first mentioned as a mill in 1140 A.D.

Although only originally a water-mill, at a later date a windmill was added, for in 1709, on the transfer of a lease one was included in the schedule — the windmill, however, did not live out the life of the water-mill, as it was not mentioned in schedules after 1872.

The mill drew its water from the Bagworth Brook, which up-stream supported Thornton Mill and down-stream, where it becomes the Rothley Brook, supported Anstey and Glenfield Mills.

Steam power was added soon after 1854, when the water flow in the brook was diminished by the formation of the Thornton Reservoir.

DISHLEY MILL

Dishley is connected with two mills in the Domesday Book. The present building, probably the smallest mill building in Leicestershire, was very well known in the past, being on the main A6 road from Loughborough to Derby, and a local rendezvous for anglers and skaters.

During the 17th Century, Dishley Mill was involved in litigation with the owners of the Loughborough Mills, being accused of violating Loughborough's soke rights by poaching customers and under-cutting prices.

The mill was not listed after 1904 in trade directories and the millpond was drained just before 1950, the mill and mill-house being converted shortly after into a very attractive private house — one of the grinding stones can be seen propped up at the front of the house.

Dishley Mill, c.1890; Miller Keightley looks on.

Dishley Mill, the wheel and wheelhouse c.1890.

DUNTON BASSET MILL

This small mill, well off the beaten track, dates back to the 13th Century, the present fine old-mill-house being Georgian. The wheel and gear are missing, but much of the timber from the mill is lying around outside. It stands at the foot of a bank, above which the old mill pond was situated — the height of the bank suggests the wheel could well have been of the over-shot type.

A Sale catalogue of 1918, when the mill, along with 42 acres of land, was sold by Charles Berridge (also owner of Broughton Astley Mill), shows it fetched £1,125. The mill then had two pairs of grinding stones and it was said about the mill that 'a good grinding business had been done for many years'.

The mill building is now being converted to form an extension to the old mill-house, which is a private dwelling.

Dunton Basset Mill and millhouse prior to renovation.

ENDERBY MILL

This mill, which drew its water from the River Soar, was working until 1957. In 1963 the wheel and gear were removed (some of it is now to be found in the windmill at Kibworth), and the mill building converted to a pigeon loft. The wheel was an all iron one around 14 feet in diameter, and of the under-shot type; it produced some 40 h.p. and drove two pairs of stones.

This site is ancient, a mill being mentioned in the Domesday survey, which presents a continuous tenancy of nearly 900 years — the surviving building dates from the mid 19th Century.

Leslie Syson features the mill in his book, *British Watermills*, having visited the mill at the time it was being cleared.

An old price list for the mill, for 1957, shows the cost of grinding 1/3 cwt. of grist (animal foodstuff) as 1s.3d.

Enderby Mill showing the original roof.

Enderby wheel just before it was dismantled for scrap.

GLENFIELD MILL

Along with Dishley, this red brick mill is one of the smallest mills in Leicestershire. It was mentioned in the Domesday Book (1086 A.D.) and successive mill buildings have been in occupation at Glenfield until the early 1900's, when the then miller, Fred Faulkner, moved to the Gilmorton Windmill. The mill stands directly on a rivulet, originally called Fulbrook — now known as the Rothley Brook, opposite a new industrial estate just outside the village, its current use being as a store for agricultural equipment. The wheel and wheel-house, as well as the sluice-gates, have been removed. Traces can still be seen, however, which suggest the wheel was one of the under-shot type and would have been approximately 14 feet diameter and 4 feet 6 inches wide.

HEATHER MILL

Heather Mill, lying just off the Heather to Ibstock road, is another of
the mills on the River Sence. Reputed to be a Domesday mill site, it
was one of the local beauty spots, being featured on many early post-
cards.

The over-shot wheel, no longer there, was sited outside the mill and
was 12 feet in diameter and 8 feet wide. The wheel powered two pairs
of grinding stones, as well as a winnowing machine and a roller mill.
The wheel developed 36 horse-power and was said to be the most
powerful in Leicestershire in its time.

The mill ceased working in 1931 and by 1938 the mill dam had been
drained and the water course changed. All the machinery was taken out
during the last war in 1941/2 by the Ministry of Supply (the fate of
many Leicestershire water-mills), presumably as part of the war effort
for scrap metal. All that remains is the ivy-clad hulk of the mill building, which now acts as a store.

*Heather Mill, early 20th Century, with brickworks chimney
in background.*

HELP-OUT MILL, ODSTONE

Help-out Mill is situated on the River Sence midway between Shacker-stone and Odstone, the name Help-out being a corruption of 'hell pot'.

There has been a mill on the site since 1313 A.D. and in the hands of the Timms family from 1734 to 1970, when the mill ceased working. Initially the Timms were tenants but bought the mill with 152 acres of land in 1818, for £1,000. The mill was then described as being 'in full trade with a stream that will work about 15 hours in 24 throughout the year'.

Originally the mill had an over-shot wheel, but in 1860 a steam engine was installed, which ran until 1902, when a turbine was put in by W. R. Bell & Co.

It is believed that Help-out Mill was the last water driven mill in Leicestershire supplying flour, sold under the name 'Sence' Self-Raising Flour — an example of the flour bag is shown as the Frontispiece.

HUNCOTE MILL

This mill building, dating from the early 19th Century, is situated on the Thurlaston Brook, a tributary stream of the River Soar, just south of the village, off the Huncote to Croft Road.

The site is an ancient one, being mentioned in the Domesday survey of 1086 A.D.

One of several Leicestershire mills to take an early advantage of steam power, it was described in 1846 as a 'large steam and water driven corn mill' — the steam chimney can be seen on the photograph. For steam enthusiasts, the boiler, I am reliably informed, was one of the Cornish type.

The wheel and mill machinery were removed in the late 1950's for scrap — the all iron water-wheel was approximately 7 — 8 feet in width, 12 — 13 feet in diameter, one of the breast-shot type, and drove three (possibly four) pairs of grinding stones.

Iron sluice gate — Huncote Mill.

HUSBANDS BOSWORTH MILL

This out-of-the-way mill, mentioned in the Domesday Book, is situated between the Welford Arm (off the old Grand Junction Canal) and the River Avon. There is a 'pull-in' on the canal where barges loaded and unloaded, and the line of a cart track can be seen leading down to the mill building. The mill building is integral with the farmhouse, for which it now acts as a store. A small building outside was formerly a bakery and at one time there was a steam engine (the site can be seen on the extreme right of the photograph). The wheel and machinery have now gone, but the wheel was probably the over-shot type. After grinding cattle food in its later years as a mill, it stopped working in 1910 and was not occupied as a dwelling house until late 1950's.

A collection of old agricultural machinery lies in the surrounding field, many items of which are still used from time to time.

LEIRE MILL

This old mill building stands off the Leire to Dunton Basset road, on a tributary steam of the River Soar, less than half a mile downstream from Dunton Basset Mill.

Now converted for private accommodation, the mill and adjoining mill-house were built in 1773.

The mill machinery is no longer there, but the wheel must have been 12 — 13 feet in diameter, judging by marks on the old wheel-house wall, and probably of the breast-shot type.

Leire Mill, in its latter working life, before the water course was altered about forty years ago, was always short of water to drive the wheel. Dunton Mill, as previously said, was less than half a mile upstream, so that when that was working the miller at Leire often had to wait up half the night before he could do his grinding.

LONG WHATTON MILL

The mill stands by the Long Whatton Brook, just outside the village. First mentioned in 1452, the present building was built in 1773 and has three storeys plus a dormer. The wheel has now gone, but was of the pitch-back over-shot type and must have been about 16 feet diameter and 14 feet wide. There appeared to have been three pairs of grinding stones, the mill only ever being involved in cereal grinding. No water now flows through the mill, it having been diverted into the main brook. The mill was worked until the 1930's by Mr. Bates, although it was not listed in Kelly's Trade Directory after 1912.

Apparently planning permission was sought to turn the mill into a restaurant, but this was refused on grounds of insufficient access. The mill is now in a derelict state, many timbers and part of the roof having collapsed.

The Stone-nut and drive into the grinding tun, wherein the grinding stones are found — Long Whatton Mill.

Long Whatton Mill, c.1890.

LOWER MILL, COTES, NR. LOUGHBOROUGH

This mill, which stands in a prominent position on the River Soar, just south of the village of Cotes, was associated with another mill which stood barely half a mile up the river and called, appropriately, Upper Mill. These two mills were the subject of disputes throughout the 17th Century because local tenants were bound to take their corn to the mills for grinding, but in 1697 a judgment was made which allowed the tenants to use Dishley or Garendon Mills.

The mill had two 18 feet diameter wheels and a 30 h.p. oil engine to assist. It ceased grinding flour in the 1950's but continued grinding animal foodstuff until 1973, being the last working water-mill in Leicestershire.

An ancestor of ex-Goon Spike Milligan, Thomas Kettleband, was killed in an accident at the mill in 1861, when his arm was caught on the wheel, which took him round 50 to 60 times before stopping, mutilating him fatally.

Lower Mill, Cotes, nr. Loughborough, c.1890.

MARKET BOSWORTH MILL

Market Bosworth Mill, first mentioned in the 13th Century, is one of the smaller mills in Leicestershire. Of striking design, it resembles a small chapel and is reminiscent of Bourne Mill (National Trust) at Colchester. It is situated just north of the village on the Measham road. It drew its water from two streams, one of which was the Barlestone Brook, a tributary stream of the River Sence.

The present building was built around 1700, using local stone from the Carlton quarry.

In the sale of the Market Bosworth Estate in 1883, the mill dam pond was shown to cover one acre and the rent to be £70 per annum.

The mill was worked by the Stanton family for three generations up until 1931 — at that time the mill had a wooden breast-shot wheel and four pairs of grinding stones — Lester Maides took over until 1939. The mill changed hands twice more before it was closed as a mill in 1957/8.

The mill building was then used as a stable for many years by the owner, until, in 1974, it was converted into an interesting and unusual private dwelling.

Market Bosworth Mill, c.1950.

Miller Drackley dressing the stones at Market Bosworth Mill, c. 1957.

PACKINGTON MILL

Another of the mill sites mentioned in the Domesday Book, Packington Mill is situated in a delightful spot on the northern edge of the village, alongside the Gilwiskaw Brook.

The mill buildings, which include a small cottage, are of red brick with a slate roof. Inside the mill the machinery can still be found — including the 14 feet diameter wood and iron water-wheel, which is of the over-shot pitch-back type, and two pairs of grinding stones. Dry rot, however, has taken over inside the mill, which makes it extremely dangerous to enter.

The mill ceased working in 1947, when the mill dam banks burst and, as the cost of repair was not an economic proposition, the mill pond was drained and the mill fell into disuse.

During the last war the owners considered renovating the mill for living accommodation, but were prevented by the £100 limit imposed during the war on such expenditures.

RATCLIFFE-ON-THE-WREAKE MILL

The mill at Ratcliffe-on-the-Wreake is picturesquely situated just south of the village on the Rearsby road.

There has been a mill at Ratcliffe since Domesday times, when one mill worth 3 shillings was mentioned. The present mill was built in 1816 using bricks made from locally dug clay. Four pairs of grinding stones were installed — an increase of two pairs on the previous mill. In 1870 a steam engine was installed for use when the water was insufficient to drive the all iron breast-shot wheel, and later four pairs of steam rollers were installed to complement the grinding stones.

The mill ceased operating in the late 1950's and is believed to have been the last water-mill in Leicestershire grinding flour using only a wheel for power.

In recent years the mill building has been extensively renovated and converted into a private dwelling, while retaining the old machinery and wheel.

Ratcliffe-on-the-Wreake Mill, prior to conversion to a private dwelling.

REARSBY MILL

One mile up-stream from Ratcliffe Mill on the River Wreake, Rearsby Mill lies tucked away down a track off the Ratcliffe to Thrussington road.

Resebi (Rearsby) was said to have two and a half mills in the Domesday survey.

The mill pond was a favourite haunt for week-end anglers, and punts were used to take sacks of flour to Ratcliffe village.

The mill had a steam stack and engine house for auxiliary power, which are now demolished, but the all iron water-wheel, which was of the breast-shot type, is still in place.

The present mill, dating from 1825, ceased operating commercially in the late 1930's and finally ceased working in the late 1940's. There was also a bake-house at Rearsby which produced a 100% wholemeal loaf, which had quite a reputation locally.

Rearsby Mill, c.1933; Miller Warden looks on.

Rearsby Mill, c.1933, Miller Warden and help loading sack onto punt for transporting to Ratcliffe.

SHEEPY MILL, SHEEPY PARVA

One of the relatively few Domesday mill sites in the west of the County, Sheepy Mill is an imposing structure standing prominently on the Sheepy Magna to Sheepy Parva road. Probably the largest old mill building in Leicestershire, the buildings now lie largely empty.

The mill, which took its water from the River Sence, had a breast-shot wheel of about 14 feet diameter in the early 19th Century. This was then replaced by a water-turbine and later by a steam engine. Early in the 1930's the power supply was changed to electricity.

New buildings adjoining the old mill are now used for grinding animal foodstuff and the old mill buildings are planned to be demolished in the near future.

SHEPSHED MILL

This ancient mill site was mentioned in the Domesday survey and further reference was made in the 13th Century in connection with the Convent of St. Mary de Pratis.

The present mill building is integral with a farmhouse and looks to date back to the early 19th Century. The wheel, made of iron with wooden vanes, is 15 feet diameter and 6 feet wide and is of the pitchback type. The mill gearing is unusual, in that there is no main shaft, instead the pit wheel drives a cog wheel at each side, both of which in turn drive two bevelled gears on parallel shafts, and these in turn, via other bevelled gears on the shafts, drive the four bevel geared stonenuts. The other mill machinery was driven via a pulley, also driven directly from the pit wheel.

The last miller was Bob Bowley, who took over the mill in 1911 and worked it until 1939. He was also a wheelwright and ran a timber saw off the mill. His father was miller at Shepshed before him, from 1900—1911. The mill was in working order in 1939, but the sluice-gates were taken down for scrap shortly after, leaving the V-shaped mill race dry.

The unusual drive at Shepshed Mill showing pit-wheel and spur-gears which are driven directly from it.

Sack hoist — Shepshed Mill.

SIBSON MILL

This small mill, which lies just off the road from Sheepy Parva to Wellsborough, drew its water from the River Sence. It is sited about one and a half miles up river from the larger Sheepy Parva Mill.

The mill was in use until about 1940, after which time it degenerated quickly, it now being used as a store.

The wheel, which has gone, appeared to be of the under-shot type, about 14 — 15 feet in diameter. Several other items of mill machinery, however, are still there, including the large wooden sack hoist pulley in the still intact grain store. The mill had two pairs of grinding stones, one pair of which were French burr.

SILEBY MILL

Two mills are mentioned in connection with Sileby in the Domesday survey (1086 A.D.). The current site was almost certainly one of the original sites and the present red brick buildings look to date from the 18th Century with 19th and 20th Century additions. The latest addition, a square wheel-house, can be seen on the extreme left of the building — this was built to house a new wheel.

The mill ground corn until the end of the 19th Century but was used latterly as a leather mill until it ceased operation around 1936. The wheel and gear have all gone, but the wheel-housing suggests a wheel of around 14 feet diameter and five foot six inches wide. The mill stands in a particularly lovely spot on the River Soar, with a canal lock and basin alongside. It is said that several people have been drowned in the basin.

Sileby Mill early 20th Century, showing steamstack.

SPITAL MILL, LUTTERWORTH

The Spital Mill lies on the River Swift just south of Lutterworth, on the Rugby road. The site could be the one mentioned in connection with Misterton in the Domesday survey as one is not mentioned at Lutterworth.

Many disputes arose between the Spital Mill and Lodge Mill, which was situated downstream on the River Swift, concerning the encroachment by the miller of Spital Mill on the rights of Lodge Mill. In 1631 agreement was reached that the grain could be taken to the Spital Mill if, within 24 hours of it being taken to Lodge Mill it was not ground.

The corn mill ceased operating in the 1890's when the building of the Great Central Railway cut off the water supply. The wheel and gear have all gone except a sack hoist on the first floor; the old sluice gate has also been dismantled and the water-way filled in. The mill was situated in the section immediately behind the mill house.

Sluice gate, Spital Mill, the buildings behind are barns some 30/40 yards from the Mill, c. 1892.

Spital Mill, Lutterworth, c.1892, just before it ceased operating.

STAPLEFORD

This unusual looking mill building stands by the River Eye in the grounds of Stapleford Park, just off the road from Stapleford to Saxby, and was for many years, until recently, hidden behind a veil of trees.

Stapeford (Stapleford) was mentioned in the Domesday survey in connection with two mills rendering eight shillings. It is probable that one of the mills was situated on the present mill-site. Another part of the park is known as the 'Melon ground', which is thought by Lord Gretton to be a corruption of 'milling ground' and could therefore be the other Domesday mill-site.

It seems unlikely that the mill, which looks to date from the late 18th Century, was worked after around 1840. It has long been converted to a dwelling house but is prone to flooding, despite the recent removal of the nearby weir. This has rendered the building uninhabitable and it is to be demolished in the near future.

STONTON WYVILLE MILL

Another of the Domesday mill sites in Leicestershire, Stonton Wyville was listed as having two mills in 1086.

The mill was still working in 1846, the power being provided by an under-shot water-wheel which drew its water from the Stonton Brook, a tributary stream of the River Welland. The mill is believed to have ceased working by 1863.

The mill machinery was located in the right-hand end of the building, which dates from the 17th Century. Additions were made to the western end of the building in the early 18th Century and the unusual mansard roof added in the late 18th Century.

STEMBOROUGH MILL

This former corn-mill is now, as the photograph shows, a private house, having been restored and renovated with obvious care. The wheel and grinding gear still remain intact on the ground floor, although partitioned off. The wheel appears to have been of the over-shot type and possibly pitch-back. The gearing which drove the two pairs of grinding stones was unusual in that no spur-wheel was used — instead the pit-wheel drove two bevelled gears which each, in turn, via another gear wheel, drove the stone-nuts. Some idea of the drop in water can be gained from the bank alongside the house, the mill race being at the top.

Interestingly, it is said that Stemborough Mill was involved in the first electrical experiments in the district. The mill ceased working in the early 1940's.

STRETTON MILL

This old mill is situated in a picturesque setting just off the main A444 road at Stretton en le Field.

The wheel, which was of the under-shot type, was sited at the extreme left of the building. The original building extended only as far as the chimney on the right, the front gables and extension to the right of the chimney only being added about ten years ago when the building was extensively and tastefully renovated. A stable for two horses formerly stood at the right end of the mill, but this was pulled down when the water course was changed to prevent flooding.

A brick in the older part of the mill shows the date of the building to be 1633. The site, however, was mentioned in the Domesday Book as having a mill, but was listed under Derbyshire.

The mill was working until around 1938.

Stretton Mill — just prior to conversion to a private dwelling.

SOAR MILL, SUTTON IN THE ELMS

Soar Mill is the first water-mill on the Soar River proper, situated near the junction of the A46 and the Sapcote turn.

The mill had a breast-shot wheel about 13 feet in diameter and six feet wide.

The mill ceased working as a water-mill in about 1934, the mill building being used for the manufacture of tyres during World War II, and then used for hosiery manufacture. It is now a thriving antique business.

TEMPLE MILL, NEAR WELLSBOROUGH

One of the smallest mills in Leicestershire, Temple Mill drew its water from the River Sence. The derivation of the name is apparently linked with the Knights Templar, with whom the surrounding land was associated.

Always used for the grinding of cereal crops, the mill was not listed in Kelly's Trade Directory after 1916 and so, presumably, fell into disuse shortly after. The Crown Lands Commissioners' Agent purchased the mill just before the Second World War, the wheel and machinery being dismantled soon after.

The wheel appeared to be of the breast-shot type and about 13 feet in diameter — there is evidence in the wheel-house of an earlier wheel which looked to have been of the under-shot type. The water course is now blocked and the mill pond filled in — only the peeping tail-race exit proclaiming its old associations.

THORNTON MILL

Another Leicestershire mill well off the beaten track, Thornton Mill stands at the bottom of a small valley on the edge of the old village.

It was first mentioned in 1279 A.D., when Anthony le Bek owned a water-mill and windmill there. The present mill building is thought to lie on the same site, although the windmill was burnt down in the late 19th Century.

The latest building was constructed in 1847 by the miller, Joseph Christian — an old beam removed from the mill and incorporated in a renovated barn proudly records the fact.

The mill drew its water from a stream off the Rothley Brook and had an over-shot wheel, which finally stopped turning in the 1930's. Shortly after, in 1935, the mill building was converted into a private dwelling house, the last miller's wife living there still.

THRUSSINGTON MILL

Another of the mills on the River Wreake, Thrussington Mill stands in a picturesque spot about one and a half miles up the river from Rearsby Mill, down a track off the Thrussington to Hoby road.

The site is mentioned in the Domesday Book and, in all probability, has been in continuous use since.

One of the smaller mills in Leicestershire, this former corn mill ceased operating around 1910. The iron gear was taken out during World War II, the only gear remaining now being the all wooden spur-wheel and main shaft.

The wood and iron wheel was of the under-shot type, about 12 feet diameter and five feet wide, and apparently drove three pairs of grinding stones.

ULVERSCROFT MILL

This old corn-mill, built of stone with a slate roof, is hidden in some private woods, alongside a public footpath from Newtown Linford to Ulverscroft. The roof of the three-storey building has all but fallen in and is in a dangerous condition.

The wheel, which was of the over-shot type and would have been approximately ten feet diameter and four feet six inches wide, has now gone and the gear lies in disarray, covered with many season's leaves. The wheel was situated at the extreme right of the building, the tail-race disappearing underground, to emerge some 100 feet away, where it joined the main stream.

The mill was in the hands of the Draper family from the early 1890's, when Joseph Draper moved from Belton Mill, until it ceased working some time between 1936 and 1941.

WORTHINGTON MILL

This fine old mill building is within sight of the now demolished Worthington Railway Station, on the old L.M. & S.R. line, just north of the village.

The earliest reference to this mill is in connection with a whirl-wind which terrorised the district in 1660, when a 'great log' from the mill-pond was lifted and whirled about.

The building is of limestone (possibly Carlton), with a slate roof, and is now used as a store. The gear was taken out around 1960, when the mill dam-pond was filled in (foreground of photograph). It had a large breast-shot wheel of 14 — 15 feet diameter and 7 — 8 feet in width.

The mill was last worked by the Chester family, who also worked the mill at nearby Belton.

Worthington Mill, around 1960, before the mill-pond was filled in.

Chapter Five

THE VANISHED WATER-MILLS OF LEICESTERSHIRE

Many of Leicestershire's water-mills have long since disappeared, very often leaving sparse record of their passing. The following lists those mills that have left a mark — however small. I visited some thirty of these sites where some trace still exists — a sluice-gate, a mill-pond, a few bricks — often these are the only clues to their former occupation.

Belgrave Mill, c.1790.

ALTON GRANGE	mentioned in the Domesday survey of 1086 as having one mill.
ASFORDBY	had two mills in Domesday times, but in modern times had one mill, the wheel of which was removed for scrap in 1932.
AYLESTONE	four mills were listed in the Domesday survey. Aylestone corn mill added a steam engine in the early 19th Century and had four pairs of grinding stones. The mill was still operating in the early part of this century but is now demolished.
BARKBY THORPE	one mill listed in the Domesday survey.
BARROW-ON-SOAR	was demolished in 1938 after a long history. Latterly used for grinding gypsum, although formerly a corn mill. Had two large wheels, 15 feet and 20 feet in diameter. Listed in the Domesday survey as having three mills.

Asfordby wheel, just before demolition.

Aylestone Mill and Locks, c.1890.

BELGRAVE	purchased by the Council in the 1890's to obtain water rights and demolished shortly afterwards. Listed as having one mill in the Domesday survey.
BIRSTALL	listed as having two mills in the Domesday survey, Birstall mill was a corn mill and believed to be still operating at the beginning of this century as a leather mill.
BOTTESFORD	listed as having seven mills in the Domesday survey. One of these sites would probably have been Easthorpe, which operated into the 1950's — the mill-house survives as a private dwelling.
BRADGATE	was situated adjacent to the ruin in the Park (see illustration Page 119).
BRAUNSTONE	listed as having two mills in the Domesday survey.
BRINGHURST	water-mill mentioned in the 12th Century.

Barrow-on-Soar Mill, early 20th Century.

BROOKSBY	a Domesday mill site still operating in the middle of the 19th Century.
BRUNTINGTHORPE	listed as having a water-mill in the Domesday survey.
BURNTDOWN MILL	aptly named, this mill on the River Sence had an over-shot wheel and was burnt down during the 17th Century.
BURTON OVERY	a water-mill mentioned in the 15th Century.
CALDWELL	two mills listed in the Domesday survey.
CARLTON CURLIEU	a water-mill mentioned in the 16th Century.
CATTHORPE	listed in the Domesday survey as having one mill.
CHARLEY	a mill was operating here in the early 19th Century.
CHURCH LANGTON	listed in the Domesday survey as having one mill.

CONGERSTONE	listed in the Domesday survey as having one mill and shown as still having a mill on Greenwood's map of Leicestershire in 1825.
COSTON	listed as having one mill in the Domesday survey, was still operating in the 19th Century and included in W. E. Cook's *Leicestershire Views.* The outline of the building can still be seen.
COTESBACH	listed as having one mill in Domesday times, it was also mentioned in 1607 and shown on Greenwood's 1825 map; it is probably the mill that became known as Lodge Mill, Lutterworth, famous for the murder of its miller in the early 17th Century.
CRANOE	a water-mill mentioned in the 13th and 14th Centuries.
CROFT	possibly the first water-mill in Leicestershire, Croft had two mills in Domesday times.

Coston Mill, c.1890.

Garthorpe Mill prior to demolition.

Garthorpe Mill and mill-pond, a favourite haunt for bathers.

CROXTON KERRIAL	listed as having two mills in Domesday times.
EARL SHILTON	listed as having one mill in the Domesday survey.
EAST NORTON	listed as having two mills in the Domesday survey.
EASTON	a water-mill mentioned in the 12th Century.
EVINGTON	listed as having one mill in the Domesday survey.
EYE KETTLEBY	believed to have ceased operating during World War I, the mill was purchased by the local Council in the early 1920's to obtain control of the water rights.
FRISBY-ON-THE-WREAKE	a Domesday mill site, Frisby mill was still operating at the beginning of this century.
GADDESBY	two and a half mills listed in the Domesday survey, one site of which is possibly the site of Ashby Folville Mill.
GALBY	a Domesday mill site, Galby mill had ceased to operate by 1610.

Eye Kettleby Mill, c.1850.

Frisby-on-the-Wreake, c.1900.

GARTHORPE	was demolished in the late 1950's, although it ceased working some years earlier — apparently a favourite haunt for bathers in times gone by.
GREAT GLEN	listed as a Domesday mill site, the mill ceased operating shortly after 1885; the mill house survives as a private dwelling.
GROBY	a water-mill is shown on Greenwood's map of 1834.
HOBY	an ancient mill site which ceased operating during the 18th Century — the weir and other remains can still be seen.
HOLYOAKES	listed as having one mill in the Domesday survey, it was not mentioned after the early 14th Century.

A view of Kings Mills, Castle Donington, early 20th Century.

HUGGLESCOTE	the last mill was rebuilt in 1797 and demolished about 15—20 years ago by the local Council.
INGARSBY	listed as a mill in the Domesday survey.
KEGWORTH	a Domesday mill listed under Sudton (Sutton Bonnington) and this is believed to be the Kegworth site on the River Soar. Was a corn mill until about 1790 when it became an iron forge mill. It quickly reverted to corn milling in about 1810 and continued in that trade until about 1870 when it began grinding gypsum. The mill closed in 1904, the mill buildings then being used for the making of baskets until about 1950. The buildings are now virtually all gone, although the old mill grinding stones still survive in the vicinity.
KILBY	listed as having one mill in the Domesday survey.

KINGS MILLS,
CASTLE DONINGTON
a Domesday mill site, Kings Mills is one of the best known of the old Leicestershire mills. Was at various times a corn, paper, fulling and finally a gypsum grinding mill. A fire closed the mill in 1927. Ref:*Historical Account of the Ancient Kings Mills at Castle Donington* (1960).

KNIGHTON
a water-mill mentioned in the 12th Century.

KNIPTON
listed as having seven mills in the Domesday survey and shown on John Prior's map of 1779 as still possessing one.

LAUGHTON
thought to be a water-mill in the 16th and 17th Centuries.

LEICESTER
possessed two mills at the time of the Domesday survey, one of these was possibly the mill that became known as Castle Mill. Castle Mill was first mentioned as such in 1301, when another of the Leicester water-mills was built, known originally as New Mill and later Newarke Mill, until in the 17th Century it

Castle Mill, Leicester, demolished 1890's.

became known as Swan's Mill after the then miller. Castle Mill ceased to function as a mill about 1876, when the weir was removed but the building was used until 1893 as a hosiery trimming factory. Newarke or Swan's Mill was demolished in 1893, until which time it was working as a flour mill. One of the other old water-mills in Leicester was North Mill, which dated from the beginning of the 12th Century. Around 1876 the water rights were acquired by the Corporation in connection with flood prevention, as a result water power could no longer be used and a steam engine was installed by 1888, the mill then continued as a corn mill until about 1905 when it was closed. St. Mary's Mill is thought to be the mill mentioned in the Domesday survey in connection with Bromkinsthorpe. It is thought to have been a corn and fulling mill until about 1799, when it was rebuilt and became a hosiery mill. It had reverted to corn grinding by the early 19th Century but in 1877 passed into the hands of an elastic-net manufacturer.

LODDINGTON a Domesday mill site, milling was carried out there into the present century — the mill is now demolished.

LOWESBY listed as having one mill in the Domesday survey.

LUBBENHAM a water-mill is mentioned in the early 16th Century.

MEASHAM a mill is mentioned in the 19th Century as having a large oak wheel, 26 feet in diameter — there were two mills indicated on Prior's map of 1779.

MELTON MOWBRAY listed as having two mills in the Domesday survey, the name of Melton it is suggested derived from Mill Town. A mill was still working on the River Eye in the 19th Century.

MOUNTSORREL a well documented mill, Mountsorrel was probably one of the three mills listed under Barrow-on-Soar in the Domesday survey. The

Mountsorrel Mill, c.1912.

Mountsorrel Mill, c.1912.

mill ceased operating around 1912, when it had two wheels, both 12½ feet in diameter, four pairs of French stones, two pairs of Peak stones and a wide range of mill equipment. The mill building was finally demolished in 1960 after having the top storey removed in the late 1940's.

NARBOROUGH
there is mention of a mill in the mid-13th Century and in modern times a mill apparently stood on the present site of the railway goods station.

NEWTON HARCOURT
listed as having one mill in the Domesday survey, but not mentioned by 1332.

NORTH KILWORTH
listed as having one mill in the Domesday survey. The last mill was demolished in 1947.

PEATLING MAGNA
listed as having two mills in the Domesday survey.

PECKLETON
traces still exist of a water-mill at Peckleton, which was certainly operating in the 19th Century.

Ravenstone Mill, during demolition in 1974.

PICKWELL	listed as having a water-mill in the Domesday survey — not mentioned after 1247 A.D.
QUENIBOROUGH	listed as having a water-mill in the Domesday survey.
QUORN	believed to be one of the three mills listed under Barrow-on-Soar in the Domesday survey, in the 14th Century it was mentioned as a fulling mill. A mill was still operating in Quorn, near Quorn House Park, up until the late 19th Century.
RATBY	one mill mentioned in the Domesday survey.
RAVENSTONE	had an over-shot wheel and was worked until about 1930; it was finally demolished in 1974.
ROTHLEY	one mill mentioned in the Domesday survey.
SADDINGTON	one mill mentioned in the Domesday survey, Saddington is shown as still possessing a mill in a trade directory of 1864.
SALTBY	two mills mentioned in the Domesday survey.
SAPCOTE	one mill mentioned in the Domesday survey.
SAXBY	two mills mentioned in the Domesday survey.
SCALFORD	a mill mentioned here in the 12th Century, and again in the 16th Century.
SHACKERSTONE	mill demolished when the railway was built in 1870.
SHAWELL	one mill mentioned in the Domesday survey.
SKEFFINGTON	one mill mentioned in the Domesday survey.
SOUTH CROXTON	one mill mentioned in the Domesday survey.
SPROXTON	three mills mentioned in the Domesday survey.
STANFORD	shown as possessing a mill on Greenwood's map of 1825.
STAPLETON	it is believed that there was a mill here in the 19th Century.
STOCKERSTONE	listed as possessing one mill in the Domesday survey, it was not mentioned after 1685.
STOUGHTON	possessed a water-mill in 1341, but this had gone by the 15th Century.
SWEPSTONE	first mentioned in the 13th Century when it was given to Nuns at Polesworth, Warwickshire.

SWINFORD	listed as having one mill in the Domesday survey.
SWITHLAND	disappeared under the waters of the Swithland reservoir in 1894.
SYSTON	listed as possessing one mill in Domesday times, the mill, which was formerly a corn mill (in 1606 — 'so scant was wind and water that people came from Hinckley to grind their corn'), had by around 1908 changed to the manufacture of fibrous board.
THEDDINGWORTH	listed as having two mills in the Domesday survey, Prior's map of 1779 still showed Theddingworth as having two mills, although only the sites are shown on a map of 1830 as Mills Close and Mill Holme.

Syston Mill, c.1890.

THORPE ARNOLD	listed as possessing one mill in the Domesday survey.
THORPE LANGTON	a mill is mentioned in 1278 A.D.
THORPE PARVA	listed as possessing a mill in the Domesday survey.
THRINGSTONE	this former corn mill was last worked around 1930 and was demolished in 1934/5.
THURCASTON	had one mill in the Domesday survey. The last mill ceased working around the time of World War 1; it is now demolished, although the foundation still remains.
THURMASTON	possessed one mill in Domesday times. Was operating as a corn mill into the 1920's but was demolished by 1930, when the site was taken over by boat builders.

Thurcaston Mill, c.1890.

Thurmaston Mill and locks, early 20th Century.

ULLESTHORPE	listed as having one mill in the Domesday survey.
UPPER MILL, COTES	probably one of the two sites mentioned in the Domesday survey, Upper Mill was closely associated with the nearby Lower Mill. The mill dam pond was blown up in 1898 to relieve flooding.
WALCOTE	listed as having one mill in the Domesday survey.
WANLIP	listed as having one mill in the Domesday survey.
WELBY	listed as having one part of a mill in the Domesday survey.
WELFORD	a mill was sited alongside the Welford arm of the Grand Union Canal.

117

Upper Mill, Cotes, nr. Loughborough, c.1890.

WELHAM listed as having a water-mill in the Domesday survey. The mill is mentioned again in 1220 A.D.

WHETSTONE possessed a mill in Domesday times.

WITHERLEY first mentioned in 1265 A.D., this mill had a long tradition. The mill was last worked in the 1920's but not commercially. The wheel was of the under-shot type and about 12½ feet in diameter. It was demolished in the late 1950's.

WISTOW listed as possessing a mill in the Domesday survey.

WYFORDBY possessed two mills in Domesday times.

WYMONDHAM the outline of foundations of a water-mill site has been located here.

Old Mill Bradgate Park, c.1841.

Distributed by
Harveys Bookshop Ltd
Leicester